The Risks of SOCIAL MEDIA

SOCIAL MEDIA ***Hate Speech***

Andrea C. Nakaya

ReferencePoint Press®

San Diego, CA

ReferencePoint Press®

About the Author

Andrea C. Nakaya, a native of New Zealand, holds a BA in English and an MA in communications from San Diego State University. She has written and edited numerous articles, and more than fifty books, on current issues. She currently lives in Eagle, Idaho, with her husband and their two children, Natalie and Shane.

Printed in the United States

For more information, contact:
ReferencePoint Press, Inc.
PO Box 27779
San Diego, CA 92198
www.ReferencePointPress.com

LIBRARY OF CONGRESS CATALOGING-IN-PUBLICATION DATA

Names: Nakaya, Andrea C., 1976- author.
Title: Social media hate speech / by Andrea Nakaya.
Description: San Diego, CA : ReferencePoint Press, [2021] | Series: The risks of social media | Includes bibliographical references and index.
Identifiers: LCCN 2020014231 (print) | LCCN 2020014232 (ebook) | ISBN 9781682828557 (library binding) | ISBN 9781682828564 (ebook)
Subjects: LCSH: Social media--Juvenile literature. | Online hate speech--Juvenile literature.
Classification: LCC HM742 .N3495 2021 (print) | LCC HM742 (ebook) | DDC 302.23/1--dc23
LC record available at https://lccn.loc.gov/2020014231
LC ebook record available at https://lccn.loc.gov/2020014232

Contents

How Social Media Is Uniquely Suited to the Spread of Hate Speech

Social media is a normal part of life in countries all over the world. India is no exception. People there use a variety of different social networking sites to connect with others; however, the most popular is WhatsApp. According to BBC News, more than 400 million Indians use this messaging app. Most WhatsApp messages are harmless chat, but as on all social media, some posts are meant to deceive or do harm. In 2018 several WhatsApp users began to circulate false stories about child kidnappers. Within hours these rumors spread to tens of thousands of users, and many people believed them. In response, violent mobs gathered in some Indian towns, and dozens of innocent passersby where attacked, with some left seriously injured and others dead.

Thirty-two-year-old Mohammad Salman was one of the victims of this mob violence. He and two friends were visiting relatives in the small village of Handikera in July when they were brutally beaten.

"They kept hitting us, demanding to know how many children we had kidnapped,"[1] Salman says. One of Salman's friends died from his wounds. Other victims were killed in similar attacks, including the lynching of five men that month. The men were poor traveling workers, one group targeted by the rumors. A previous false message about a child abduction plot in May said a transgender woman was involved, and convinced crowds beat a transgender woman to death in response. The BBC reported in July that at least seventeen people had died since the various rumors began that April.

This frightening incident shows the unique power of social media to quickly and powerfully affect a large number of people. It took just hours for a few hateful messages on WhatsApp to spread through a region, targeting specific—usually marginalized—groups. In this case the hateful messages had so much power that they caused large groups to take violent action in several communities. While hate speech is nothing new, social media hate speech is relatively new, as new as social media. Hate speech on social media is different because social media has qualities that make it uniquely

An Indian family grieves over the death of a relative who was killed by an angry mob inflamed by false reports of child kidnappings that were published on the social networking site WhatsApp.

suited to the spread of hateful messages. As the WhatsApp-related incident in India shows, hateful rhetoric can spread quickly and seem even more convincing when it spreads through social media.

The Ease of Posting and Accessing Hate Speech on Social Media

Hate speech is any form of communication that expresses threatening or discriminatory views toward a specific group of people. While hate speech can occur for any reason, people are most commonly targeted on the basis of race, ethnicity, gender, religion, sexual orientation, disability, or age.

Hate speech can be nonverbal. For example, the Nazi swastika symbolizes racial hatred, and Germany bans its display as it has been deemed a form of hate speech. It is not surprising to find hate speech on social media, because these platforms accommodate both words and images.

The design of social media can make people more likely to post hateful messages and can also make it easier for those messages to spread. The simplicity of posting comments, for example, makes it easy to impulsively speak without considering the real consequences of that speech. Social media users generally interact on their phones or other electronic devices—not in person—and sometimes they even do so anonymously. This means that when people use social media, they may feel more protected from the reactions they might otherwise get if they made inconsiderate comments in person. Tech blogger Jamie Bartlett says, "It is true that hiding behind a screen allows—sometimes maybe encourages—people to say and do things they wouldn't in person. And the increase in nasty, offensive, and in certain cases clearly illegal, behaviour online is a big problem."[2] In some cases users do not even realize how much harm their hate

> "It is true that hiding behind a screen allows—sometimes maybe encourages—people to say and do things they wouldn't in person."[2]
>
> —Jamie Bartlett, tech blogger

causes, because they do not necessarily understand that a careless or intentionally hostile remark directed toward another user can be read and passed on by everyone who sees that post.

Social networks also allow hate groups to grow because it is so easy to connect with other people who believe the same thing. Jason Bloom is a partner at a law firm that specializes in social media cases. He explains, "Whereas, pre-internet, a person with hateful viewpoints may have struggled to identify others sharing such viewpoints, the Internet and social media make it easier for such people and groups to find each other."[3] Furthermore, as Zachary Laub explains in a research paper for the Council on Foreign Relations, the statistical algorithms that social media sites use actually push users toward finding others who share their interests and beliefs. He says, "Online platforms' business models depend on maximizing reading or viewing times. Since Facebook and similar platforms make their money by enabling advertisers to target audiences with extreme precision, it is in their interests to let people find the communities where they will spend the most time."[4]

A Powerful Way to Spread Messages

In addition to connecting users who share similar interests, social media also spreads messages to large numbers of people who might not otherwise be exposed to those messages. One of the most distinctive things about hate speech on social media is the sheer number of people that it can reach. Without social media, many people would not be in contact with the individuals and groups who have hateful things to say. However, with social media, anyone with access to an electronic device such as a phone or computer can post a hateful message and broadcast it to people all over the world. The Dangerous Speech Project's senior researcher, Cathy Buerger, comments that this allows people with certain speech norms—or ways of speaking—to be exposed to ideas outside those norms. She says, "With social media, speech . . . can easily be discovered and broadcast to a larger audience that doesn't share the same speech norms." Overall, she says, "This speech becomes more visible than it otherwise would have been."[5]

> "With social media, speech . . . can easily be discovered and broadcast to a larger audience."[5]
>
> —Cathy Buerger, a senior researcher at the Dangerous Speech Project

Finally, hate speech on social media can spread unnoticed and affect a lot of people before anybody does anything about it. Taylor Lorenz, a reporter for the *Atlantic*, talks about how this happens on the social media site Instagram. Lorenz explains that Instagram users can set their accounts as private, which means that their content can only be accessed by approved users. She says:

> Instagram relies on users to report problematic content, and . . . a lot of extremists' memes, for instance—you might have a meme page with 10,000 followers—all of those people are very susceptible to white nationalist beliefs and the account is set to private. So, it's kind of what we're seeing with Facebook groups too, where there's no outside person policing it. This type of stuff is not appearing on a lot of normal users' feeds.[6]

As a result of this lack of policing, hate on social media can grow and extend its influence without anyone to stop it.

As social media remains increasingly popular throughout the world, critics wonder about the risks of hate speech on the ever-expanding variety of social media platforms. In the United States free speech is protected under the First Amendment, and only crimes can be prosecuted, not offensive words. As a result, what to do about hate speech on social media has been left primarily to the companies that control the various platforms. However, society continues to worry about hate speech on social media and wonder whether the current situation needs to change. Experts debate exactly how hate speech on social media affects individuals and society. Similarly, commentators argue about whether companies or the government can—or should—do anything to regulate that speech.

Is Hate Speech on Social Media a Serious Problem?

Brandon Farbstein has a rare form of dwarfism. In 2014, at age fourteen, he joined the social media site Instagram to help educate people about his condition. In an interview with *Atlantic* reporter Taylor Lorenz, he explains that he wanted to "show people a glimpse into my life and inspire people."[7] What he got in response was a staggering amount of hate. Explains Lorenz, "The hateful messages started coming: death threats, expletive-laden comments about his appearance, worse. A meme page put his face on Hitler's body."[8] The hate got so bad that Farbstein says he started to fear for his safety to the point that he had to leave school and do online school instead. "It's draining, it's anxiety producing," Farbstein says, "I'm used to people calling me names, but it's when people say that they're going to kill me or come find my family that really gets me in a sense of pure terror."[9] He says that the Instagram harassment ruined high school for him.

Farbstein's experience is not unique. Research indicates that hate is common on most social media sites. That hate comes in many forms, from hateful statements to death threats like those Farbstein received. Overall though, most people agree that hateful comments are widespread on social media. What they disagree on is whether it is a serious problem. Some people believe that social media hate is a serious threat to the well-being of both individuals and society, while others contend that its potential harms have been greatly exaggerated.

Hate Speech on Social Media

The Pew Research Center has been tracking social media use since 2005, and it reports that 72 percent of Americans are on at least one social media platform. Reliance on social media is not unique to the United States; the use of social media is steadily increasing all around the world. Media company We Are Social predicts that by the end of 2020, more than half of the world's population will be consumers of social media. While there are a variety of different platforms,

The use of social media is increasing around the world. We Are Social predicts that by the end of 2020, more than half the world's population will be using social media

and most people use more than one, some of the most common are Facebook, YouTube, Instagram, Snapchat, Twitter, Pinterest, and WhatsApp. According to Pew Research, in 2019, 69 percent of US adults used Facebook, and about 75 percent used YouTube. A large percentage of social media users are on these various sites daily, and many are spending a significant amount of time there. For instance, according to a 2019 report by the market research company GlobalWebIndex, internet users spend almost two and a half hours a day using social networking and messaging platforms.

Many of these users are coming across hate speech in their daily social media feeds. A national reporting initiative called News21 documents the variety of hate speech arising on social media in the United States. In one of its reports, journalist Kianna Gardner gives some specific examples of online hate that she has seen:

> On Twitter, David Duke, former Grand Wizard of the Ku Klux Klan, sometimes tweets more than 30 times a day to nearly 50,000 followers, recently calling for the "chasing down" of specific black Americans and claiming the LGBTQ community is in need of "intensive psychiatric treatment." On Facebook, James Allsup, a right-wing advocate, posted a photo comparing migrant children at the border to Jewish people behind a fence during the Holocaust with the caption, "They present it like it's a bad thing #BuildTheWall." On Gab, a censorship-free alternative to Twitter, former 2018 candidate for U.S. Senate Patrick Little, claims ovens are a means of preserving the Aryan race. And Billy Roper, a well-known voice of neo-Nazism, posts "Let God Burn Them" as an acronym for Lesbian Gay Bisexual Transgender.[10]

Gardner's examples show just a few of the ways that hate speech is disseminated on social media.

Often people who have hateful beliefs identify with particular hate groups. A hate group is a group of people who share certain hateful beliefs. The Southern Poverty Law Center (SPLC) monitors hate groups in the United States. While it notes that some groups espouse a variety of ideologies, it lists the major categories of hate groups as falling under certain affiliations: Ku Klux Klan, neo-Nazi, white nationalist, racist skinhead, Christian identity, neo-Confederate, black nationalist, anti-immigrant, anti-LGBT, and anti-Muslim. Some target specific minority groups—such as blacks, Jewish people, immigrants, or queer communities—while others vent their hatred against multiple victims. Overall, the SPLC estimates that there are currently 1,020 hate groups operating in the United States, nearly all of which have representation on social media.

A Common Experience

Caroline Knorr, parenting editor for Common Sense Media, argues that online hate speech is so widespread that most social media users will encounter it at some point, even if it is not directed at them. She especially focuses on young people, saying, "The vast majority of kids will be victims of everyday, casual exposure. Just by playing a game on the internet, looking up a definition, or maybe checking out some music, they'll encounter some of the most vile and offensive words and images that can be expressed in the comments section of a YouTube video, a meme in their feed, or a group chat."[11] News21 analyzed the social media activity of a number of hate groups in the United States over a two-week period in 2018 and found that these groups were circulating a large quantity of hateful content that was being seen by many kids and adults. In just two weeks the hate groups they tracked had more than 3 million followers

> **"The vast majority of kids will be victims of everyday, casual exposure [to online hate]."[11]**
>
> —Caroline Knorr, parenting editor for Common Sense Media

Teens may encounter hateful content on social media merely by trying to access music through online sources.

combined, made over twenty-five hundred posts, got more than half a million likes, and had their posts shared almost two hundred thousand times.

Surveys of social media users also confirm that hate is common on social media. For example, in 2018 the Anti-Defamation League surveyed more than one thousand Americans and found that more than half had experienced hate speech or other types of harassment online. The survey revealed that social media users view hate speech as a serious problem; 59 percent of those surveyed said they thought online hate and harassment are making hate crimes more common, and 22 percent said online hate is making them feel less safe in their community. Further, the majority believed that the problem is serious enough to require action by both social media companies and the government. Anti-Defamation League chief executive officer (CEO) Jonathan A. Greenblatt comments, "It's deeply disturbing to see how prevalent online hate is, and how it affects so many Americans."[12]

Do Not Overlook the Benefits of Social Media

Social media has made it easier than ever before for people to spread hateful messages, and that has caused a lot of worry. However, some people argue that society should not focus so much on the potential harms of online hate that it forgets that social media has also had some very positive effects. Nadine Strossen, a law professor at New York Law School and the author of *Hate: Why We Should Resist It with Free Speech, Not Censorship*, talks about some of the benefits of social media. "Just as you get more hate speech through these new technologies, you also have much more effective response to hate speech," she points out. In addition, she reminds users that social media enables the spread of positive messages too. She says, "The other speech going on is incredibly inspiring. You could not have had the social-justice movement, from Black Lives Matter to #MeToo and the anti-gun movement. They really flourished thanks to social media." Strossen and many others insist that it is important not to get so caught up in the potential negatives of social media hate speech that these many positives are forgotten.

Quoted in Knowledge@Wharton, "How Can Social Media Firms Tackle Hate Speech?," September 22, 2018. https://knowledge.wharton.upenn.edu.

The Presence of Hate Groups on Social Media

While some hate speech on social media comes from individuals—for instance, hateful comments on other users' posts—hate groups also have a presence on these platforms. There is evidence that by using the power of social media to spread their messages and attract new followers, many of these hate groups are becoming increasingly strong. Researchers led by Neil F. Johnson of the George Washington University studied hate group networks on social media and found strong, tech-savvy, and interconnected communities that were very resilient to any attempts to stop the spread of their messages. The researchers observe, "Interconnected hate clusters form global 'hate highways' that . . . cross social media platforms, sometimes using 'back doors' even after being banned, as well as jumping between countries, continents and languages."[13] Not only did the researchers find that hate groups have a strong social media presence, they also observed that when attacked—for instance, if one of their pages is shut down—these groups are very good at rewiring and repairing their networks.

There is also some evidence that social media is not just allowing hate groups to grow but is helping them make their messages more acceptable to mainstream society. For example, Lorenz says that she has seen a large number of Instagram posts that contain hateful content and have been widely viewed and liked. She gives an example of @the.new.federation, an America First group on Instagram: "@the.new.federation . . . has more than 38,000 followers. . . . Yesterday, it asked, 'If Muslims can behead Christians, why can't we do the same to them?' That post has 2,088 likes."[14]

The British antifascism advocacy group Hope Not Hate warns that in recent years hate group messages have moved from existing on the fringes of society to being more and more common in the mainstream. For example, Hope Not Hate says that anti-Muslim prejudice is more commonly voiced by mainstream political and media figures than it was only a few years ago. The group warns that this new trend is a real threat because it means that hate has more power than ever before. It explains, "It is far easier to challenge the hate of a small group, especially when its views are considered unacceptable by the mainstream." However, says Hope Not Hate, many hate groups now use social media to become larger and more popular in the mainstream, meaning that they are more difficult to challenge. It says, "Islamophobia is on the rise [and] antisemitism is reappearing and other forms of hate crimes are also on the increase. We are facing challenges on more fronts and in different ways than ever before."[15] Hope Not Hate believes that hate has become so prevalent that it is infecting politics and mainstream media and leading to greater social division.

While fears like this are common, on the other side of the debate are those people who point out that the nature of social media makes it possible for large amounts of hate speech to be erased. Unlike many other types of hate speech, hate speech on social media can be deleted instantly. It is argued that not only do social media companies have the ability to delete hate speech, they are actively doing so. George Washington University professor Amitai Etzioni argues that, in fact, social media companies are censoring too much hate speech and other content. "Actually, as I see it, over the last few years the tech corporations have blocked or deleted staggering amounts of messages and ads," he says, "including material which, if removed from offline publication, would lead even moderate defenders of free speech to go ballistic."[16]

Because social media platforms are owned by private companies, however, these businesses have the right to delete this content if they choose to. Niam Yaraghi, a fellow at the Brookings Institution, argues that in deleting large amounts of hate speech, social media companies are doing the public a favor. He says, "Private regulators are doing what government officials may not do: regulating and suppressing speech believed to cause harm to citizens generally and protected groups specifically."[17]

The Harms of Hate Speech

Another point of disagreement regarding social media hate speech is the effects it has on the people exposed to it. Many people insist that hate speech can cause serious harm to those who encounter it. Greenblatt says that people experience online hate and its many harms every day and that its effects linger. He believes that online hate can be so powerful that sometimes it forces people to change their habits in order to avoid that hate. "Cyberhate is not limited to what's solely behind a screen; it can have grave effects on the quality of everyday lives—both online and offline,"[18] he states. The organization ConnectSafely agrees, explaining that individuals, communities, and society can all experience real harm from hate speech on social media. ConnectSafely argues that this harm can

> "The targets of hate speech can experience negative emotional, mental, and physical consequences. These can include low self-worth, anxiety, fear for their lives, and even self-harm or suicide."[19]
>
> —ConnectSafely, an organization concerned with online safety

Hate speech can cause emotional, mental, and physical problems in those who encounter it.

occur in numerous ways. Individually, it says, "the targets of hate speech can experience negative emotional, mental, and physical consequences. These can include low self-worth, anxiety, fear for their lives, and even self-harm or suicide."[19] However, the organization also insists that hate speech harms whole communities and society because it damages the relationships that people have with one another and their ability to empathize with each other.

While most Americans are in favor of free speech rights, surveys show that many people believe that hate speech on social media is so harmful that it should be against the law. Nadine Strossen, author of *Hate: Why We Should Resist It with Free Speech, Not Censorship*, is not in favor of censorship; however, she reports that many people are. She says, "Public opinion surveys and other data, going back to the mid-twentieth century, consistently demonstrate that most people simultaneously hold two inconsistent notions of free speech. On the one hand, when asked about freedom of speech in the abstract, most people are supportive. After all, freedom of speech is a cherished national value 'as American as apple pie.'" However, she says that many people make an exception when it comes to hate speech. "When

The Lingering Harms of Hate Crimes

Researchers believe that hate crimes have different effects on victims than other types of crimes. In a hate crime individuals are not attacked at random; instead, they are targeted specifically because of an aspect of their perceived identity, such as race or religion. This means that victims of hate crimes often feel vulnerable—at the moment of the crime and afterward—because they cannot change the thing about them that inspired the attack. Hate crimes can also affect communities in a similar way. The Anti-Defamation League says, "Hate crimes have an impact that lingers, and extends beyond the specific victim. They make members of minority communities fearful, angry and suspicious, and raise tensions that can divide and polarize neighborhoods, towns and cities."

Anti-Defamation League, "#50StatesAgainstHate: An Initiative for Stronger Hate Crime Laws," 2020. www.adl.org.

asked about freedom of speech for particular controversial views," she says, "many of the very same people favor censorship."[20]

A 2019 poll by the Campaign for Free Speech found that 48 percent of those surveyed believed that hate speech should be against the law. Of these, more than half believed that possible jail time would be an appropriate punishment for anyone found guilty of spreading hate speech. In a 2019 survey by the tech and media company Morning Consult, researchers found that of the different types of content that people find most objectionable on social media, hate speech ranks first. The majority of the people in that survey said that they believe social media companies should be forced to remove hate speech on their platforms.

Harms of Social Media Have Been Exaggerated

Some people argue that while hate speech on social media can be upsetting, fears about its harms are greatly exaggerated. Milton Mueller is a professor at the Georgia Institute of Technology's School of Public Policy and director of the Internet Governance Project. He argues that social media is not causing hate to become worse. Hate has always existed, he says, and the nature of social media is simply to make that hate speech—as with everything else on social media—highly visible to society. Mueller says:

> The human activities that are coordinated through social media, including negative things such as bullying, gossiping, rioting, and illicit liaisons, have always existed. In the past, these interactions were not as visible or accessible to society as a whole. As these activities are aggregated into large-scale, public commercial platforms, however, they become highly visible to the public and generate storable, searchable records. In other words, social media make human interactions hypertransparent.[21]

Mueller insists that this hypertransparency is leading to an unjustified panic that hate speech on social media is causing great harm to society. This kind of fear is not a new phenomenon, he notes, explaining that in the past, every time society creates a new form of media, there are fears that it will be harmful.

Weighing Benefits Against Drawbacks

Many commentators also argue that while hate speech on these platforms might cause some harm, social media also has many benefits, such as helping people share information and connect with one another. They insist that these benefits far outweigh the harms. In 2019 the Pew Research Center surveyed people around the world and found that many agree with the argument that social media has an overall positive impact. The organization surveyed people in eleven countries and reports that in seven of those countries, half or more of those surveyed believe that social media has mostly been a good thing for society.

Social media has established a strong presence in society and will not be gone any time soon. However, it is clear from the reports of its many users that hate speech also has a strong presence on social media. As a result, the debate over online hate continues in the United States and around the world, as members of society continue to disagree on whether that hate constitutes a serious problem.

Can Online Hate Speech Lead to Real-World Violence?

In 2019 suspected white supremacist Brenton Tarrant went on a shooting spree at two mosques in Christchurch, New Zealand. He killed fifty-one people and injured almost as many before he was arrested by police. According to news reports, Tarrant had online accounts that he used to post images and messages that celebrated violence against Muslims and other minorities. *Newsweek* says that prior to the shooting, Tarrant posted, "Well lads, it's time to . . . make a real life effort post. I will carry out and attack against the invaders, and will even live stream the attack via facebook . . . by the time you read this I should be going live."[22] Using a camera mounted on his head, he broadcast the first of the two shootings live on Facebook.

Tarrant is not the only person who has posted hateful messages on social media and then gone on to commit violent acts in real life. When online hatred spills out into the real world, it raises the question of whether hate speech in social media contributes to violence in the community. This is a difficult question to answer. Some people believe that the two are unrelated, while others insist that online hate speech does make real-world violence more likely.

Hate Speech and Hate Crime

The connection between social media and violence in the real world is important to consider because hate crimes are serious problems throughout the world. By understanding why hate crimes occur, researchers hope that they might be able to reduce them. As in many nations, estimates on the number of hate crimes in the United States vary; however, by any count, this type of crime is believed to be significant. The FBI reports that there are thousands of hate crimes in the United States every year, and these include property damage, assault, rape, and murder. The Bureau of Justice Statistics reports, however, that the num-

This mosque in Christchurch, New Zealand, was one of two mosques attacked by white supremacist Brenton Tarrant, who broadcast one of his attacks on Facebook.

ber actually falls in the hundreds of thousands yearly. No matter what the real number of crimes is, the fact is that a lot of people worry about becoming victims of a hate crime. In a 2019 Gallup poll, 11 percent of those surveyed said they frequently worry about being a victim of a hate crime, and 14 percent said they occasionally worry. Hate crimes occur for many different reasons, but according to the US Department of Justice's most recent report, race, ethnicity, or ancestry is the most common motivator of hate crime, causing more than half of all hate crimes reported in the United States. Next most common is religious-based hate crimes, followed by hate crimes targeting sexual orientation.

Some experts believe that hate speech on social media does lead to real-world violence at least some of the time. Heidi Beirich is director of the SPLC's Intelligence Project. She explains that hate on social media teaches people antisocial views and can then inspire them to act on those views. This is not an inborn but a learned behavior, she says: "We know people are radicalized by interacting with others to learn how to hate black people or Jews or so on."[23] Researchers at New York University investigated hate speech on Twitter and found that the rhetoric sometimes prompts individuals to turn their thoughts into deeds. Thus, the researchers suggest that there is a statistical relationship between expressions of hate and actual hate crimes. They analyzed approximately 532 million tweets posted from 2011 to 2016 that focused on race, ethnicity, and national origin, then compared the discriminatory tweets with hate crime occurrences. Lead researcher Rumi Chunara summarizes the results: "We found that more targeted, discriminatory tweets posted in a city related to a higher number of hate crimes."[24] The analysis included data from a hundred different US cities, with varying urbanization and population diversity.

Normalizing Hate

There is evidence those who embrace the messages within hate speech do so because they think that such views are common and

A Possible Correlation Between Anti-Refugee Posts and Hate Crimes

Researchers Karsten Müller and Carlo Schwarz wanted to get a better understanding of how hate on social media is related to hate crime. In order to do so, they analyzed anti-refugee statements on Facebook in relation to hate crimes against refugees in Germany. They explain that their theory was that "social media information channels can reinforce anti-refugee sentiments, which may push some potential perpetrators over the edge to carry out violent acts." They found evidence supporting this theory. The analysis revealed that during times of high Facebook usage and periods of high anti-refugee sentiment, there was an increase in anti-refugee hate crimes. The data also showed that when there were Facebook outages, there were fewer hate crimes.

Karsten Müller and Carlo Schwarz, "Fanning the Flames of Hate: Social Media and Hate Crime," SSRN, November 3, 2019. https://ssrn.com.

accepted in society. Social media can be a powerful tool in fostering this belief. Journalist Casey Newton found out just how persuasive social media can be when he interviewed content moderators for Facebook. Content moderators review posts—including posts with hateful content—to make sure they do not violate the standards set by the site, and then they make decisions about whether the posts stay up or are taken down. According to Newton, some moderators found that constant exposure to some postings changed their beliefs in ways they never would have predicted. He says:

> The moderators told me . . . the conspiracy videos and memes that they see each day gradually lead them to embrace fringe views. One auditor walks the floor promoting the idea that the Earth is flat. A former employee told me he has begun to question certain aspects of the Holocaust. Another former employee, who told me he has mapped every escape route out of his house and sleeps with a gun at his side, said: "I no longer believe 9/11 was a terrorist attack."[25]

Where Americans Experience Hate on Social Media

The Anti-Defamation League surveyed 1,134 Americans in 2018 to find out about their experiences with hate and harassment on social media. Of those people who experienced online hate or harassment, more than half said it happened on Facebook. Twitter, YouTube, and Instagram were the next most common platforms for hate and harassment.

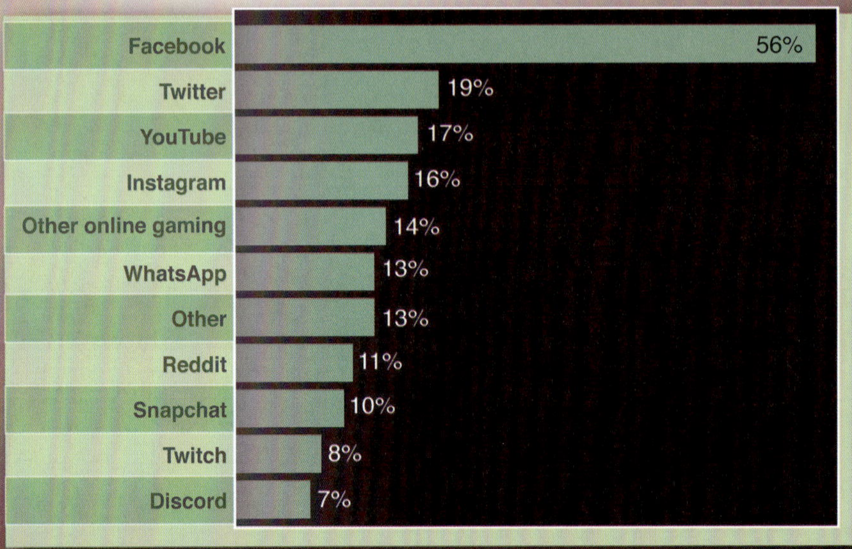

Source: "Online Hate and Harassment: The American Experience," Anti-Defamation League, 2018. https://www.adl.org/onlineharassment.

Many people believe that just as social media can cause people to change their beliefs about things like the Holocaust and the earth being round, it can also change beliefs about whether hating certain groups is justified and whether violence against those groups is acceptable and perhaps necessary.

One way that social media might affect a person's beliefs is through the sheer volume of postings that it allows. On social media, it is easy for users to put a lot of hateful messages on many platforms. By creating a continual torrent of hate speech, a person or group can make those messages seem normal and socially acceptable, especially when viewers begin to echo those sentiments by reposting or commenting positively on the hateful messages.

Researchers have found that people are heavily influenced by what they believe other people think and do. Adam Neufeld, vice president of innovation and strategy for the Anti-Defamation League, explains how hate groups use this facet of human nature to their advantage on social media. According to Neufeld, "One of the big things that changes online is that it allows people to see others use hateful words, slurs and ideas, and those things become normal. Norms are powerful because they influence people's behaviors. If you see a stream of slurs, that makes you feel like things are more acceptable."[26] Neufeld and others believe that when people are constantly exposed to hate online, they gradually begin to think that this type of speech is a normal way for people to express themselves. Furthermore, they can also come to believe that hateful action—fueled by this rhetoric—is normal too.

> "One of the big things that changes online is that it allows people to see others use hateful words, slurs and ideas, and those things become normal."[26]
>
> —Adam Neufeld, vice president of innovation and strategy for the Anti-Defamation League

Another way that hateful messages are normalized in social media is through cruel or insensitive humor. Taylor Lorenz, a reporter for the *Atlantic*, describes how some hate groups use memes and other humorous posts to draw people into their way of thinking. She explains, "Memes and humor in general disarms people and it makes them almost more susceptible to extremist beliefs. Humor is a really good way to introduce people to ideas, especially extremist ideas, and conspiracy theories." She explains how this happens subtly. "You kind of start by laughing at it," she says. "Then, you start by questioning things a little bit, and you can end up believing and getting sort of sucked up in a lot of this stuff through humor."[27] Many people are so focused on the humor that at first they may not even realize there is a hateful message present too.

Targeting Young People

Young people in particular are often the targets of attempts to normalize hate with humor and other strategies. Lorenz explains that extremist hate groups frequently target young people because they are heavy social media users and because young people are more likely to be impressionable. She says:

> It's not all young people that are following these [extremist] pages, but primarily it's a lot of teenagers, maybe college students, kids right out of school who are kind of looking to form their identity and learn about the world—learn about news events—and they're increasingly turning to social media to do that. Instagram and YouTube are the two most used platforms for Generation Z. So they're following these accounts and just becoming susceptible to their ideas.[28]

Furthermore, says Lorenz, many social media sites use algorithms to steer users toward pages similar to what they are already viewing, so if a person finds one extremist page, a social media site often makes it easy to find more.

Writer and editor Joanna Schroeder talks about how her two boys—ages eleven and fourteen—were targeted by white supremacist messages of hate in social media. After wondering about the source of some comments her boys were making, she investigated their social media activity. She says that what started as humorous memes led to an onslaught of racist, sexist, and homophobic messages. She ended up writing a series of tweets about what she found, warning other parents that their children might be unknowing targets of hate groups. Her first message was, "I've been watching my boys' online behavior & noticed that social media and vloggers are actively laying groundwork in white teens to turn them into alt-right/white supremacists."[29] Schroeder quickly discovered that her situation was not unique; she received a large numbers of responses from other parents who had noticed the same thing happening to their children.

Is the Expression of Hate a Trigger or a Safety Valve?

While some experts believe that social media can spread hate and influence viewers, there is widespread debate about whether this influence promotes hate crimes. Some insist that online hate speech is dangerous because it allows violent feelings to escalate in viewers without any consequences. Then these feelings spill over into real-world violence. Shannon Martinez formerly belonged to a white power group. She is now program director of the Free Radicals Project, which helps people get out of hate groups. She explains how violence can build up through expression on social media. "In the physical world, if you're standing in front of someone and you say something abhorrent, there's a chance they'll punch you," she says. "Online, you don't have that, and you escalate into further physical violence without a threat to yourself."[30] Martinez and others believe that this lack of consequences means that some people continue to express online

Although violence against minorities is a known problem, some critics say that there is no evidence that online hate speech translates into physical hate crimes.

hate and that this expression fuels their anger, allowing it to grow until some trigger sets it off.

However, in response to such arguments, some critics contend that while the connection might seem logical, there is no evidence to support the theory that online hate speech translates into physical hate crimes. Alexis C. Madrigal, a staff writer at the *Atlantic*, cautions that people cannot assume that hate speech circulating on social media is promoting violent crimes just because both exist. He points out that violence has many potential causes. To make his point, he discusses the WhatsApp controversy in India, in which mob lynchings followed false rumors circulated on the app. In his opinion, while WhatsApp may have played a role in circulating the hateful messages, there are other—more likely—causes for the ensuing violence. "Every serious report finds other

The Influence of Hate Speech on Social Media May Depend on Existing Attitudes

In a study of Russian social media users, researchers found that the effects of social media hate can vary depending on the beliefs that users already have. The researchers looked at how use of the popular social media site VKontakte (VK) affected xenophobic attitudes and ethnic hate crimes in Russia. Xenophobia is where a person shows prejudice against people from other countries. They found that a greater penetration of social media did lead to more ethnic hate crimes. However, this was only the case in cities that already had a high level of nationalist sentiment. To measure existing nationalist sentiment, the researchers looked at the level of support that Rodina, a nationalist and xenophobic party, received in a prior election. They explain, "The impact of social media on hate crime victims positively and significantly depends on the strength of pre-existing support of nationalists in the city: for example, a 10% increase in VK penetration increased hate crimes by 25.8% in cities where Rodina received most votes, but had zero effect in cities where Rodina got minimal support."

Leonardo Bursztyn et al., "Social Media and Xenophobia: Evidence from Russia," University of Chicago, December 2019. https://home.uchicago.edu.

deep-rooted factors, too," he explains, "The local authorities may have incited one crime because some people owed them money. In several cases, the violence drew on religious tensions. In a third the . . . myth of the *xopadhora*, or 'child lifters,' touched off the attack."[31] He cites Yaso Córdova, a researcher affiliated with the Harvard Kennedy School of Government, who is also skeptical of blaming WhatsApp for the violence in India. Córdova points out, "[People in] Italy and Spain are heavy WhatsApp users, too, but there is no conversation about whether WhatsApp incentivizes death in Italy or Spain. So I am inclined to look at other aspects of the entire ecosystem, like social and economic aspects."[32]

Others agree that there are numerous other likely causes for the hate-related violence that happens in the real world. They argue that stopping online hate is not the way to stop hate crimes. Andrew Torba, founder of social media site Gab, insists that preventing hate speech on social media does not stop violence, because it is not the speech that is causing the violence. He says, "Guns do not kill people. Social media platforms do not kill people. People kill people."[33] Or as Jonathan Rauch of the Brookings Institution contends, "The problem isn't the speech. The problem is the hate."[34] In his opinion, the best way to reduce that hate is to understand and confront it.

"If speakers—especially fringe or offensive speakers—are suppressed, they will simmer and eventually boil over and explode, destabilizing society and government."[35]

—Roy S. Gutterman, director of the Tully Center for Free Speech at Syracuse University

Some people believe that allowing the expression of hate on social media makes violence in the real world *less* likely. According to this argument, hate speech online allows people to let out their feelings without enacting real violence. This is sometimes called the "safety valve" theory. Roy S. Gutterman, director of the Tully Center for Free Speech at Syracuse University, explains, "The theory posits that if speakers—especially fringe or offensive speakers—are suppressed, they will simmer and eventually boil over and explode, destabilizing society and government. Thus, society will let speakers, even those with ugly, unpopular or

> "Blocking online activity fuels narratives of victimization and risks further isolating disaffected individuals."[36]
>
> —Danielle Keats Citron, a scholar at the Yale Information Society Project and the Stanford Center for Internet and Society

infuriating viewpoints, vent."[35] The vocal or written expression of hate is the safety valve that prevents the explosion. Thus, if people are free to engage in hate speech on social media, experts believe these individuals will feel less of a need to draw attention to their cause through violent acts.

Danielle Keats Citron is an affiliate fellow at the Yale Information Society Project and an affiliate scholar at the Stanford Center for Internet and Society. She explains how trying to block expressions of hate can backfire and cause that hate to build up to a dangerous level. "Blocking online activity fuels narratives of victimization and risks further isolating disaffected individuals," she says, "Aggrieved speakers may feel even more aggrieved and more inclined to act on pent-up anger."[36] Citron insists that the benefits of venting on social media outweigh the potential harms of letting that hatred be bottled up.

A Recurring Debate

Society continues to experience violent acts like Brenton Tarrant's shooting spree. Every time a new crime like this occurs, the debate over hate speech on social media is renewed. Yet there remains widespread disagreement over whether online hate can cause violence in the real world. Understanding the connection between online hate speech and violence is of great importance to society because it could help prevent tragic acts such as Tarrant's shooting spree and the thousands of other violent hate crimes that occur around the world every year.

Should Social Media Censor Hate Speech?

Hate on social media can cause significant harm to individuals and society. David Kaye is the United Nations special rapporteur on the promotion and protection of the right to freedom of opinion and expression. He says, "Online hate, with the speed and reach of its dissemination, can incite grave offline harm and nearly always aims to silence others." He argues that because of this potential for grave harm, society must do something to address hate on social media. "The question is not *whether* to address such abuse," he insists. "It is *how* to do so in a way that respects the rights everyone enjoys."[37] Exactly what to do is one of the most significant questions society faces. There continues to be widespread disagreement over whether there should be limits to hate speech on social media. And if so, what should they be, and who should dictate them?

Hate Speech and the First Amendment

In order to understand the debate over the censorship of hate speech in the United States, it is important to understand the First Amendment to the

"Online hate, with the speed and reach of its dissemination, can incite grave offline harm and nearly always aims to silence others."[37]

—David Kaye, United Nations special rapporteur

US Constitution. The First Amendment protects free speech, and this protection extends to nonverbal communications such as pictures and video. According to the First Amendment, the US government cannot limit free speech, even if most citizens consider something to be offensive. As Eugene Volokh, the Gary T. Schwartz Distinguished Professor of Law at the University of California, Los Angeles, explains, "The First Amendment protects all ideas, loving, hateful, or in between."[38]

The nation's founders believed that free speech is vital to preserving the free and open exchange of ideas that a democratic society depends on, and the First Amendment was written to enshrine that belief. By tolerating—though not condoning—all types of speech, the First Amendment permits society to hear and judge different viewpoints, even unpopular or hateful ones. The American people are the ones who must consider carefully what they hear or read and decide how to respond. For instance, the Foundation for Individual Rights in Education (FIRE), an organization that works to protect the rights of American college students and faculty members, explains that the First Amendment gives American citizens—not the government—the power to take action against speech that they do not like. It says, "We as citizens possess the power to most effectively answer hateful speech—whether through debate, protest, questioning, laughter, silence, or simply walking away."[39] According to the rationale of the founding fathers, it is important for citizens to make their own decisions about hate speech, not have those decisions made for them.

"The First Amendment protects all ideas, loving, hateful, or in between."[38]

—Eugene Volokh, a professor of law at the University of California, Los Angeles

This interpretation of the First Amendment has been affirmed numerous times through Supreme Court decisions, and only a few exceptions have been established. The government can limit

America's founders enshrined their belief that free speech is vital to a democratic society in the First Amendment to the US Constitution.

speech when that speech leads to a crime. For example, citizens cannot claim free speech protections in cases of libel or obscenity, in issuing fighting words, or when words threaten or incite violence. Therefore, hate speech can be punished if it entails making threats against somebody else. While the First Amendment protections are unique to the United States, the importance of protecting free speech has been widely recognized around the world, and various governments have set limits on what violates free speech protections.

The Rights of Social Media Companies

Hate speech on social media is unique because social media platforms have the right to make and enforce their own content rules and to censor—or not censor—their content if they wish. Users agree to this when they sign up for a social media account and accept the terms offered by the company. Niam Yaraghi, a fellow at the Brookings Institution, explains that social media companies have the right to free speech just as individuals do because they are protected by the First Amendment. He insists, "Social media companies are all private businesses with discretion over the content they wish to promote, and any effort by government to influence what social media platforms promote risks violating the First Amendment."[40]

The power of social media companies to control the content on their sites is also tied to the Communications Decency Act, which was passed in 1996. Jonathan Peters is *Columbia Journalism Review*'s press freedom correspondent. He explains section 230 of the act, which holds social media platforms free from ac-

The Communications Decency Act has been interpreted to mean that social media platforms such as Facebook and Twitter cannot be held liable for most of the material posted on their sites.

countability for any harms that result from hate speech or other content posted on their sites. He says:

> The law states: "No provider or user of an interactive computer service shall be treated as the publisher or speaker of any information provided by another information content provider." It also states that intermediaries don't lose their protection even if they moderate content. That means platforms such as Facebook, Twitter, and Gab [a social media site known for its far-right users], are not liable for most of their user-generated content.[41]

Peters explains that one reason for this protection is that it would be impractical for social media companies to screen the huge amount of content on their sites.

The Incentive to Monitor Hate Speech

As a result of these legal protections, most social media companies edit their content in one way or another. Currently, every social media company has its own unique policy about what kind of content is allowed and not allowed, and each company monitors and removes content according to those policies. Social media sites also remove users who violate their guidelines. Some people believe these safeguards are working to keep hate speech off most platforms. They maintain that social media companies are economically motivated to make most users on their site happy; therefore, companies will naturally censor what the largest share of the community finds offensive.

Experts point out that if a company does not adhere to community norms—for instance, discouraging speech that is hateful—then it will alienate users and see less profit. Writing in the *Harvard Law Review*, Kate Klonick explains, "If a platform creates a site that matches users' expectations, users will spend more time on the site and advertising revenue will increase." Hate speech will likely drive users and advertisers away, so companies are not inclined to protect posters' free speech and tolerate all content. As Klonick puts it, "Keeping up all content on a site risks making users uncomfortable and losing page views and revenue."[42] For this reason, Klonick and others believe that social media companies can be relied on to find the best balance between free speech and censorship for their platforms.

The Call for Additional Government Regulation

Other people disagree with the belief that social media companies should have complete control over their content, including hate speech. Instead, they argue that private companies cannot be relied on to monitor everything and that, because the issue is so important, the government needs to take a more active role in regulating online hate speech. According to a 2018 survey by the Anti-Defamation League, more than 80 percent of Americans agree. Researchers found that these Americans want additional government action in strengthening laws and policing related to hate and harassment online.

One reason many people want additional government oversight is because they believe that because it is so easy to post on social media, hate speech has become so prevalent that it is threatening the free exchange of ideas that the First Amendment was intended to protect. Richard Stengel was the US Department of State undersecretary for public diplomacy and public affairs from 2013 to 2016. He argues that the First Amendment was written when the United States did not have technology like social media. He explains, "The intellectual underpinning of the First Amendment was engineered for a simpler era." According to Stengel, "The amendment rests on the notion that the truth will win out in what Supreme Court Justice William O. Douglas called 'the marketplace of ideas.'" He adds, "The presumption has always been that the marketplace would offer a level playing field. But in the age of social media, that landscape is neither level nor fair."[43] He argues that, unfortunately, truth does not

Fighting Hate Speech with Counterspeech

Some people believe that one of the best ways to respond to hate speech on social media is through something called counterspeech. The Dangerous Speech Project defines counterspeech as "any direct response to hateful or harmful speech which seeks to undermine it." The group explains, "Just as influential speakers can make violence seem acceptable and necessary, they can also favorably influence discourse through counterspeech." Researcher Cathy Buerger talks about some of the creative counterspeech organizations she has found:

> One of my favorites is #Jagärhär, a Swedish group that collectively responds to hateful posts in the comment sections of news articles posted on Facebook. . . . On the #Jagärhär Facebook page, group administrators post links to articles with hateful comments, directing their members to counterspeak there. Members tag their posts with #Jagärhär (which means, "I am here"), so that other members can find their posts and like them. . . . Liking the counterspeech posts . . . drives them up in relevance ranking, moving them to the top and ideally drowning out the hateful comments."
> Buerger explains that she likes this strategy because it shows the power of people working together against hate.

Dangerous Speech Project, "Counterspeech," 2020. https://dangerousspeech.org.

Quoted in Daniel Jones and Susan Benesch, "Combating Hate Speech Through Counterspeech," Berkman Klein Center, August 9, 2019. https://cyber.harvard.edu.

always win when falsehoods are given equal footing in cyberspace. For example, he says that in a 2016 Stanford University study, researchers found that 82 percent of middle school students did not know the difference between a real news story and sponsored content. Additionally, a quarter of high school students were not able to distinguish between a real news site and one that had been designed to look real but was not. He concludes that in an environment in which false information can be so persuasive that it buries the truth, society may need to restrict some hate speech.

A Stanford University study found that 82 percent of middle school students cannot distinguish between real news and sponsored content. That same study found that a quarter of high school students could not tell the difference between a real news site and a fake one.

Furthermore, while free speech is a valued right in many countries, critics point out that allowing social media companies to do whatever they want may ironically be causing censorship of free speech, and this is another reason why additional government involvement in the issue might be necessary. Users of social media chat with friends, post to news groups, answer questions, react to videos and messages, and much more. All posting and sharing is controlled by social media companies, which have the freedom to withhold it or delete it if it violates a user-agreement policy. This means that social media companies have enormous power over what is said on their sites, including the power to decide what should be defined as hate speech and what types of hate speech should or should not be allowed.

Some critics worry that the companies are not held to any standard and their decisions could be easily motivated by profit. Vera Eidelman, a staff attorney with the Speech, Privacy and Technology Project at the American Civil Liberties Union, explains, "Every time Facebook makes the choice to remove content, a single company is exercising an unchecked power to silence individuals and remove them from what has become an indispensable platform." She points out that these companies can use that power to censor any topic that they choose. "For the same reason that the Constitution prevents the government from exercising such power, we should be wary of encouraging its exercise by corporations that are answerable to their private shareholders rather than the broader public interest,"[44] she says. George Washington University professor Amitai Etzioni agrees. He insists, "Protecting speech—and figuring out the rare occasions people should be denied voice, should be censored—is too important to leave to Facebook CEO Mark Zuckerberg and his fellow tech tycoons."[45] Instead, he argues that control of hate speech and other types of speech should be left to elected officials and the courts, not social media companies.

> "Every time Facebook makes the choice to remove content, a single company is exercising an unchecked power to silence individuals and remove them from what has become an indispensable platform."[44]
>
> —Vera Eidelman, an attorney at the American Civil Liberties Union

Letting Users Make Their Own Decisions

While some groups continue to disagree over who should be regulating hate speech, others contend that there should be no censorship of hate speech by either government or social media companies. They argue that there simply is no fair or just way to regulate any kind of speech. David French is senior editor of the Dispatch, a conservative online journal. He maintains that society cannot avoid bias, no matter how good the intention, and so any attempt to regulate speech can have unforeseen and harmful effects. He insists,

A Call for Greater Transparency from Social Media Companies

Most major social media companies prohibit hate speech on their platforms, and many have made public statements about how they are working hard to get rid of it through increased monitoring by both humans and computer programs. However, some critics worry that simply trying to remove hate speech is not a complete solution. Instead, they maintain that efforts to eradicate hate speech may threaten freedom of expression, so social media companies also need to improve their transparency and accountability. "As the world's biggest social media platform, Facebook's processes for removing content can have a serious impact on artists, human rights organisations, journalists and activists who rely on social media for their work and connections," explains the organization ARTICLE 19. It continues, "This is something ARTICLE 19 had first hand experience of recently, when a member of staff had their account temporarily blocked after trying to upload a video, which ironically was aimed at raising awareness of censorship by social media platforms." The organization argues that removing hate is not good enough. It insists that social media companies need to be much more transparent about exactly how they are identifying and removing hate speech and be open about how often they make mistakes.

ARTICLE 19, "Facebook must be more transparent and accountable over harmful content takedowns," January 21, 2020. www.article19.org.

"No one has a sufficient monopoly on truth to serve as philosopher king over speech and debate." Unfortunately, he says, "censors can behave in unpredictable, arbitrary, and capricious ways." Instead, he believes that the only way to avoid such bias is for users to make their own decisions about what to look at and what to delete or block. "Yes, this puts the 'burden' on individuals to click a button," he says. "But this is far preferable to putting the burden on even well-meaning men and women to regulate speech coherently, fairly, and consistently. The long history of censorship shows this is not possible. Even the brightest minds fail."[46]

Additionally, a look at the history of censorship reveals that not only are well-meaning censors inevitably biased, but societal beliefs and norms can change considerably over time. What many in society believe to be fair and just at one point in time can be seen as completely unjust years later. Civil liberties activist Nadine Strossen explains that as harmful as hate speech is, it can be even more harmful to censor it because the pendulum of what people believe to be right can swing wildly to the other side. For example, she says, "Not that shockingly long ago it was left-wing speakers, communists and socialists, who were kept off campuses. And civil rights activists were kept off many campuses, because their ideas were certainly hated, certainly seen as dangerous and insulting. And today, there are serious government officials who are saying that Black Lives Matter is a hate group." Yes, she agrees, censorship can cause serious harm: "[You can feel] threatened. You can feel emotionally disturbed. You can feel psychic trauma, which can have physiological manifestations. You can feel silenced. These are all real harms that may be suffered by people who are subject to hate speech that is not punishable."[47] However, she insists that society endures these harms precisely because it has learned that punishing the speech that causes them can do even more harm. Strossen and other defenders of free speech believe that a vital part of democracy is the fact that societal views change over time as people publicly debate different ideas. They caution that any censorship of speech will impede that process.

Making Informed Decisions

A lot of people believe that not only is it best to let individuals make their own decisions about what to read, watch, and listen to, but allowing them to do so is the best way to fight hate speech. Many argue that the most powerful way to counter hate is not to stop people from hearing it but to let them counter it with rational thought that they have accumulated by educating themselves on the issues at hand. In doing so, they can make informed decisions about what they hear or see. Danielle Keats Citron is a scholar at the Yale Information Society Project and the Stanford Center for Internet and Society. She says, "A key insight of free speech theory is that individuals need to speak and listen to make decisions about the kind of society they want. . . . Extremist and hateful speech adds valuable information to public discourse: the fact that such views exist can highlight the need to counter them."'[48] Strossen agrees. She explains that there is strong evidence backing this theory, stating, "Censorship of hate speech, no matter how well-intended, has been shown around the world and throughout history to do more harm than good in actually promoting equality, dignity, inclusivity, diversity, and societal harmony."[49] Instead, she insists that the best way to counter hate speech is through more speech.

All over the world, people continue to disagree about the best way to act in response to hate speech. Social media companies continue to censor their sites; however, their actions provoke widespread public debate. There is much concern over the harmful effects of hate speech in social media, yet at the same time, there is a lack of agreement over how best to address those effects without causing other harms, such as restricting the open public debate that is an important foundation of a free society.

What Is Being Done About Online Hate Speech?

Social media sites contain uncountable postings, with new content appearing constantly. Niam Yaraghi, a fellow at the Brookings Institution, discusses tweets in order to illustrate the magnitude of social media content. "Take Twitter," he says. "It is estimated that 500 million tweets are sent per day. Assuming that each tweet contains 20 words on average, the volume of content published on Twitter in one single day will be equivalent to that of *New York Times* in 182 years."[50] Among all that content is a significant amount of hate speech. There is extensive debate regarding what should be done about the hate in social media. Critics continue to disagree over whether social media companies are doing a good job of confronting online hate or whether they need to do more. There is also a lot of discussion over the actions governments have taken to address this issue and whether these actions have been effective in curbing the harms of hate speech.

Most Social Media Companies Prohibit Hate Speech

Hate speech is forbidden by most of the busiest social media sites. Their content rules clearly indicate that such speech is banned. These sites use three main tools to enforce their rules: user reporting, content moderators, and artificial intelligence programs. Users can report alleged hate speech directly to system administrators. Administrators then decide whether to remove the content if it infringes the site's rules. A lot of hate speech is found and removed by this type of reporting. However, most social media companies cannot rely solely on user reporting, so they hire content moderators, whose job is to find and delete hate speech or anything else that is in violation of the site's guidelines. Finally, because there is so much content to monitor on social media, most companies also use artificial intelligence programs to locate key words (or word groups) and images that are associated with hate speech

When users report hate speech to a social media site, its administrators can remove the content if they decide that it violates the site's guidelines.

and then flag them for removal. The programs learn by going through older "toxic" speech and determining patterns—even subtext—that can then be applied to assessing new postings.

> "We do not allow hate speech on Facebook because it creates an environment of intimidation and exclusion and in some cases may promote real-world violence."[51]
>
> —Facebook's community standards

Facebook is the world's largest social media company, and its content policy regarding hate speech is typical of most social media giants. The policy states: "We do not allow hate speech on Facebook because it creates an environment of intimidation and exclusion and in some cases may promote real-world violence." Hate speech is defined by the company as "a direct attack on people based on what we call protected characteristics—race, ethnicity, national origin, religious affiliation, sexual orientation, caste, sex, gender, gender identity, and serious disease or disability."[51] In 2019 the company announced further restrictions on hate speech, stating that it will not allow support, praise, or representation of white nationalism and white separatism. Organizations or individuals that violate Facebook's rules are banned from the site. If banned content is found, it is deleted.

Are Social Media Sites Doing Enough to Remove Hate Speech?

While Facebook has stated that it does not allow hate speech, thus far it has been unable to keep all hate speech off its site. This has encouraged a heated debate over whether Facebook is doing a good job of enforcing its policies on hate and even whether those policies are justified in the first place. Facebook has repeatedly defended itself, stating that it continues to improve its abilities to detect and remove content that violates its standards. In a November 2019 publication, the company reported substantial progress. It stated that from July to September 2019, about 7 million pieces of hate speech were removed and that 80 percent of that speech was found by Facebook before users reported

Using Human Rights Law as a Standard of Social Media Regulation

In the face of widespread disagreement over how social media companies should best moderate their content, David Kaye, a United Nations special rapporteur, has a recommendation. He argues in a 2018 report that companies should use international human rights law as a standard for content moderation. He explains, "Companies should recognize that the authoritative global standard for ensuring freedom of expression on their platforms is human rights law, not the varying laws of States or their own private interests." He continues, "Human rights law gives companies the tools to articulate and develop policies and processes that respect democratic norms and counter authoritarian demands." In Kaye's opinion, using human rights law is the best way to strike a balance between freedom of expression and the protection of human rights.

David Kaye, "2018 Thematic Report to the Human Rights Council on Content Regulation," United Nations Human Rights Office of the High Commissioner, 2018. www.ohchr.org.

it. The company has also shared that it is trying to stop people from seeking out hateful posts in the first place. It explains, "We'll also start connecting people who search for terms associated with white supremacy to resources focused on helping people leave behind hate groups. People searching for these terms will be directed to Life After Hate, an organization founded by former violent extremists that provides crisis intervention, education, support groups and outreach." However, Facebook admits that work remains and that it faces substantial challenges. "We also need to get better and faster at finding and removing hate from our platforms," the company says, pointing out that there are always those people who attempt to "game the system."[52] However, Facebook insists that it is deeply committed to keeping hate off its site and is making good progress in doing so.

Despite statements such as this from Facebook, many critics contend that the company is doing a poor job of enforcing its rules against hate speech. Facebook uses both algorithms and human moderators to detect and remove hate, but some argue that its rules are unevenly enforced and that it often makes mistakes when it does enforce them. For example, critics have found many cases in which one piece of hate speech is removed while something very similar is not. In 2017 the online news organization ProPublica investigated how Facebook deals with hate speech. It analyzed more than nine hundred posts and reported that Facebook content reviewers do not always follow the company's guidelines properly. Its reporters claimed, "We asked Facebook to explain its decisions on a sample of 49 items, sent in by people who maintained that content reviewers had erred, mostly by leaving hate speech up, or in a few instances by deleting legitimate expression. In 22 cases, Facebook said its reviewers had made a mistake."[53]

Time writer Billy Perrigo points out another problem with Facebook's attempts to remove hate. The company's algorithms are becoming

The artificial intelligence algorithms that Facebook relies on to identify hate speech have difficulty in India, which has twenty-two official languages.

more and more effective, he says, but they only work in certain languages. He explains, "That means it has become easier for Facebook to contain the spread of racial or religious hatred online in the primarily developed countries and communities where global languages like English, Spanish and Mandarin dominate." In contrast, in many other languages, Facebook must rely on human content moderators or Facebook users to find hate speech. What this means, Perrigo says, is "that racial slurs, incitements to violence and targeted abuse can spread faster in the developing world than they do at present in the U.S., Europe and elsewhere."[54] For example, he says that India has twenty-two official languages, but only four are covered by the algorithms that Facebook uses. This means that Facebook is not as good at finding hate speech among users in India.

Removing Hate Speech on Twitter and YouTube

Like Facebook, Twitter has rules against hateful conduct. It states that users may not attack or threaten people or promote violence based on a long list of categories, including race, national origin, ethnicity, sexual orientation, gender, age, religious affiliation, serious disease, and disability. Twitter's website defends this policy, stating, "Twitter's mission is to give everyone the power to create and share ideas and information, and to express their opinions and beliefs without barriers. . . . We recognise that if people experience abuse on Twitter, it can jeopardize their ability to express themselves."[55] Twitter says it works to prevent hate speech on its platform so that all users will have the opportunity for free expression there.

Whether Twitter is preventing hate speech is a topic of debate, however. Twitter users often report that they continue to be targeted by hate speech on the platform. Further, as with Facebook, it is often argued that Twitter mistakenly removes content that does not violate its guidelines. Jessica González is senior counsel at Free Press, an organization that works to preserve the rights of all people to connect and communicate online. She believes innocent users who comment on incendiary topics sometimes

> "Twitter needs to do a wholesale reform of its content moderation policy."[56]
>
> —Jessica González, senior counsel at Free Press

fall victim to Twitter's anti–hate speech algorithms and moderators. "People are being taken down who are protesting racism and people are staying up who are wildly racist and organizing racist rallies using social media and using Twitter, in particular," she says. "Twitter needs to do a wholesale reform of its content moderation policy."[56] Jack Dorsey is the cofounder of Twitter. He contends that while Twitter's content moderation may not be perfect, users also need to play a role in keeping hate speech off Twitter. He says, "A lot of the calls for 'remove the Nazis' are also due to the fact our enforcement operates on reporting. A lot of people

Twitter cofounder Jack Dorsey says that users have an obligation to help keep hate speech off social media platforms.

don't report. They see things, but it's easier to tweet out 'get rid of the Nazis' than to report it."[57] Other critics agree with Dorsey that users have an obligation to help get hate off social media platforms.

YouTube is another major social media site that prohibits hate speech. It has continued to update its policies on hate content and improve its efforts to police that content. YouTube prohibits content that promotes violence or hatred against groups or individuals, based on a list of categories similar to those of Twitter and Facebook. Individuals violating YouTube's policy are warned for a first violation, then after three strikes their channel is deleted. According to YouTube, the company has been actively investing in the resources it needs to protect its viewers from hate, and it says that these efforts have been effective. "Thanks to these investments, videos that violate our policies are removed faster than ever and users are seeing less borderline content and harmful misinformation,"[58] the company states.

However, like Facebook and Twitter, YouTube faces many criticisms of its efforts to keep hate speech off its platform. When it announced its most recent efforts to more effectively curb hate speech, writer Sarah Perez reacted with skepticism. "Policies like this sound good on paper," she explains, "but enforcement is still YouTube's biggest issue. YouTube has around 10,000 people focused on controversial content, but its decisions to date have seen it defining what's 'harmful' in the narrowest of ways. It's unclear if this tightening of policies will actually impact what YouTube actually does, rather [than] what it says it will do."[59] Critics insist that despite YouTube's efforts, it is still pretty common to encounter hateful content on the platform.

Government Actions to Prevent Hate Speech

Social media companies are not the only entities attempting to reduce online hate. Several different governments have also taken various actions to stop hate speech on social media. Germany has taken decisive legal action. In 2017 it passed a law under

A Slippery Slope

Some people fear that government attempts to force social media companies to remove hate are pushing society down a slippery slope that will lead to more and more censorship of social media content. Human rights experts Jacob Mchangama and Joelle Fiss discuss the example of Germany, where new laws require social media companies to remove hate speech within twenty-four hours of finding it. Mchangama and Fiss argue that Germany's laws have inspired other countries to follow its example but with much greater restrictions. They state, "Several of these countries, including Venezuela, Vietnam, India, Russia, Malaysia, and Kenya, require intermediaries to remove vague categories of content that include 'fake news,' 'defamation of religions,' and 'anti-government propaganda,' and many of them include overly broad definitions of hate speech that go much further than the German law." They worry that such restrictions are extremely harmful to freedom of expression.

Jacob Mchangama and Joelle Fiss, "Germany's Online Crackdowns Inspire the World's Dictators," *Foreign Policy*, November 6, 2019. https://foreignpolicy.com.

which social media companies with more than 2 million registered users in Germany must remove hate speech from their sites within twenty-four hours of finding it or risk being fined. In 2019 Germany issued its first fine under the law; Facebook was fined 2 million euros ($2.3 million). In 2020 Germany moved toward creating even greater restrictions on hate speech in social media. Under a proposed new law, social media companies would be required to report criminal postings like hate speech to the police.

Other nations are trying to force social media companies to remove more hate speech as well. In 2019 Australia passed the Sharing of Abhorrent Violent Material Act. The law was created in response to the Facebook livestreaming of the mosque shooting in New Zealand, which occurred that same year. The 2019 act creates criminal penalties for social media companies that do not quickly remove inappropriate material such as the footage of the shooting. Many other countries have also proposed or passed laws that will make social media companies more accountable for hate speech on their sites. For instance, in India—where hate on social media was linked to some serious real-world violence—new rules have been proposed under which social media platforms would have to take down content that the government deems inappropriate. Pakistan is also trying to implement similar regulation. Some countries have even temporarily banned access to social media to stop hateful messages. For example, Sri Lanka did so in 2019 after a series of terrorist attacks there.

Regulation Is Controversial

Government regulation of social media content has been very controversial. Critics of regulation fear that hate speech is not the only thing that will be censored on social media and that government censorship is reducing overall freedom of expression. In addition, Yascha Mounk, author of *The People vs. Democracy: Why Our Freedom Is in Danger and How to Save It*, warns that censorship laws often have the opposite effect of what is intended. They sometimes provide a rallying point for extremist groups that claim governments are becoming too powerful. He says, "These kinds of laws often actually strengthen the resolve of those on the right, giving them a convenient narrative about how they . . . are the oppressed ones." He cites the German anti-immigrant group Alternative for Germany as an example, explaining, "The far-right populist party Alternative for Germany, in particular, has long claimed that it is being censored (a tactic that helped propel it into the Bundestag [federal parliament] for the first time last fall [2017], when Alternative for Germany won 94 seats)."[60] In Mounk's view, government attempts to eradicate hate speech do not work and only end up making these groups more powerful.

> **"These kinds of laws often actually strengthen the resolve of those on the right, giving them a convenient narrative about how they . . . are the oppressed ones."[60]**
>
> —Yascha Mounk, author

Yet despite fears about the effects of government regulation, many people steadfastly believe that government action is working. Some people again point to Germany. As a result of the country's strict stance against hate speech, many social media users report that they are finding less hate speech online. For instance, according to news reports, Twitter users in Germany encounter less hate speech now that the government has imposed strict laws. Jillian York of the Electronic Frontier Foundation says, "It's absolutely true that there's less Nazi content available here [in Germany]."[61] As a result, many have changed their Twitter account locations to Germany so that they can use the platform without encountering so much hate.

Overall, there continues to be extensive disagreement over whether enough has been done to address the presence of hate on social media. Many people argue that even when pushed to do so by government regulation, social media companies have failed miserably in addressing expressions of hate on their sites, evidenced by the fact that it is still easy to find a large quantity of hate on social media. However, others contend that these criticisms are missing the point. They argue that society should not be trying to eliminate all hate from social media, because it is impossible to do so, there or elsewhere. Instead, it is argued that future efforts should focus more on providing social media users with views that counter the hateful messages they see. The only certainty is that social media will continue to grow, and as a result, hate speech will likely continue to trouble users, companies, and governments as more and more messages of all kinds fill these popular platforms of expression.

Introduction: How Social Media Is Uniquely Suited to the Spread of Hate Speech

1. Quoted in BBC News, "How WhatsApp Helped Turn an Indian Village into a Lynch Mob," July 19, 2018. www.bbc.com.
2. Jess Phillips and Jamie Bartlett, "Should Anonymous Social Media Accounts Be Banned?," *The Guardian* (Manchester), September 30, 2018. www.theguardian.com.
3. Quoted in Heather Leighton, "Online Hate Report Sheds Light on Prevalence of Social Media Hate," *Forbes*, August 28, 2019. www.forbes.com.
4. Zachary Laub, "Hate Speech on Social Media: Global Comparisons," Council on Foreign Relations, June 7, 2019. www.cfr.org.
5. Quoted in David Jones and Susan Benesch, "Combating Hate Speech Through Counterspeech," Berkman Klein Center, August 9, 2019. https://cyber.harvard.edu.
6. Quoted in Korva Coleman, "Instagram Has a Problem with Hate Speech and Extremism, 'Atlantic' Reporter Says," *All Things Considered*, NPR, March 30, 2019. www.npr.org.

Chapter One: Is Hate Speech on Social Media a Serious Problem?

7. Quoted in Taylor Lorenz, "Instagram Has a Massive Harassment Problem," *Atlantic*, October 15, 2018. www.theatlantic.com.
8. Lorenz, "Instagram Has a Massive Harassment Problem."
9. Quoted in Lorenz, "Instagram Has a Massive Harassment Problem."
10. Kianna Gardner, "Social Media: Where Voices of Hate Find a Place to Preach," Hate in America, News21, August 15, 2018. https://hateinamerica.news21.com.
11. Caroline Knorr, "Where Kids Find Hate Online," *Parenting, Media, and Everything In Between* (blog), Common Sense Media, August 5, 2019. www.commonsensemedia.org.

12. Quoted in Anti-Defamation League, "More than One-Third of Americans Experience Severe Online Hate and Harassment, New ADL Study Finds," February 13, 2019. www.adl.org.
13. Neil F. Johnson et al., "Hidden Resilience and Adaptive Dynamics of the Global Online Hate Ecology," *Nature*, August 21, 2019. www.nature.com.
14. Taylor Lorenz, "Instagram Is the Internet's New Home for Hate," *Atlantic*, March 21, 2019. www.theatlantic.com.
15. Nick Lowles, ed., "State of Hate 2020: Far Right Terror Goes Global," Hope Not Hate, February 2020. www.hopenothate.org.uk.
16. Amitai Etzioni, "My Experience with Social Media Restrictions on Free Speech," *National Interest*, December 15, 2019. https://nationalinterest.org.
17. Niam Yaraghi, "Regulating Free Speech on Social Media Is Dangerous and Futile," *TechTank* (blog), Brookings Institution, September 21, 2018. www.brookings.edu.
18. Quoted in Anti-Defamation League, "More than One-Third of Americans Experience Severe Online Hate and Harassment, New ADL Study Finds."
19. Brittan Heller and Larry Magid, "Parent's and Educator's Guide to Combating Online Hate Speech," ConnectSafely, 2019. www.connectsafely.org.
20. Nadine Strossen, "Counterspeech in Response to Changing Notions of Free Speech," American Bar Association. www.americanbar.org.
21. Milton Mueller, "Challenging the Social Media Moral Panic: Preserving Free Expression Under Hypertransparency," Cato Institute, July 23, 2019. www.cato.org.

Chapter Two: Can Online Hate Speech Lead to Real-World Violence?

22. Quoted in Jason Murdock, "8chan User Claiming to Be New Zealand Shooter Posted 'See You All in Valhalla' Before Mosque Massacre," *Newsweek*, March 15, 2019. www.newsweek.com.
23. Quoted in Jasmine Garsd, "Free Speech or Hate Speech: When Does Online Hate Speech Become a Real Threat?," NPR, November 19, 2018. www.npr.org.
24. Quoted in New York University Tandon School of Engineering, "Hate Speech on Twitter Predicts Frequency of Real-Life Hate Crimes," June 24, 2019. https://engineering.nyu.edu.
25. Casey Newton, "The Trauma Floor," The Verge, February 25, 2019. www.theverge.com.

26. Quoted in Rachel Hatzipanagos, "How Online Hate Turns into Real-Life Violence," *Washington Post*, November 30, 2018. www.washingtonpost.com.
27. Quoted in Coleman, "Instagram Has a Problem with Hate Speech and Extremism, 'Atlantic' Reporter Says."
28. Quoted in Coleman, "Instagram Has a Problem with Hate Speech and Extremism, 'Atlantic' Reporter Says."
29. Joanna Schroeder (@iproposethis), "I've been watching my boys' online behavior," Twitter, August 12, 2019, 12:20 a.m. https://twitter.com.
30. Quoted in Hatzipanagos, "How Online Hate Turns into Real-Life Violence."
31. Alexis C. Madrigal, "India's Lynching Epidemic and the Problem with Blaming Tech," *The Atlantic*, September 25, 2018. www.theatlantic.com.
32. Quoted in Madrigal, "India's Lynching Epidemic and the Problem with Blaming Tech."
33. Quoted in Garsd, "Free Speech or Hate Speech."
34. Quoted in Garsd, "Free Speech or Hate Speech."
35. Roy S. Gutterman, "When Free Speech Devolves into Violence," Syracuse.com, August 17, 2017. www.syracuse.com.
36. Danielle Keats Citron, "What to Do About the Emerging Threat of Censorship Creep on the Internet," Cato Institute, November 28, 2017. www.cato.org.

Chapter Three: Should Social Media Censor Hate Speech?

37. Quoted in United Nations Human Rights Office of the High Commissioner, "Governments and Internet Companies Fail to Meet Challenges of Online Hate," October 21, 2019. www.ohchr.org.
38. Eugene Volokh, "The 3 Rules of Hate Speech and the First Amendment: Episode 2," *Reason*, February 19, 2019. https://reason.com.
39. FIRE, "Mission." www.thefire.org.
40. Yaraghi, "Regulating Free Speech on Social Media Is Dangerous and Futile."
41. Jonathan Peters, "How the Law Protects Hate Speech on Social Media," *Columbia Journalism Review*, November 2, 2018. www.cjr.org.
42. Kate Klonick, "The New Governors: The People, Rules, and Processes Governing Online Speech," *Harvard Law Review*, April 2018. https://harvardlawreview.org.
43. Richard Stengel, "Why America Needs a Hate Speech Law," *Washington Post*, October 29, 2019. www.washingtonpost.com.

44. Quoted in Sasha Ingber, "Facebook Bans White Nationalism and Separatism Content from Its Platforms," NPR, March 27, 2019. www.npr.org.
45. Etzioni, "My Experience with Social Media Restrictions on Free Speech."
46. David French, "Law & the Courts: The Social Media Censorship Dumpster Fire," *National Review*, March 1, 2019. www.nationalreview.com.
47. Quoted in NPR, "Free Speech vs. Hate Speech," June 5, 2018. www.npr.org.
48. Danielle Keats Citron, "What to Do About the Emerging Threat of Censorship Creep on the Internet."
49. Quoted in NPR, "Free Speech vs. Hate Speech."

Chapter Four: What Is Being Done About Online Hate Speech?

50. Niam Yaraghi, "How Should Social Media Platforms Combat Misinformation and Hate Speech?," *TechTank* (blog), Brookings Institution, April 9, 2019. www.brookings.edu.
51. Facebook, "12: Hate Speech," 2020. www.facebook.com.
52. Facebook, "Standing Against Hate," March 27, 2019. https://about.fb.com.
53. Ariana Tobin et al., "Facebook's Uneven Enforcement of Hate Speech Rules Allows Vile Posts to Stay Up," ProPublica, December 28, 2017. www.propublica.org.
54. Billy Perrigo, "Facebook Says It's Removing More Hate Speech than Ever Before. But There's a Catch," *Time*, November 27, 2019. https://time.com.
55. Twitter, "Hateful Conduct Policy," 2020. https://help.twitter.com.
56. Quoted in Dell Cameron, "Civil Rights Groups Mostly Unimpressed by New Twitter Policy Against 'Dehumanizing' Language," Gizmodo, July 9, 2019. https://gizmodo.com.
57. Quoted in Brian Hiatt, "Twitter CEO Jack Dorsey: The *Rolling Stone* Interview," *Rolling Stone*, January 23, 2019. www.rollingstone.com.
58. YouTube, "Our Ongoing Work to Tackle Hate," *Official Blog*, June 5, 2019. https://youtube.googleblog.com.
59. Sarah Perez, "YouTube's Tougher Harassment Policy Aims to Address Hate Speech, Veiled Threats and Repeat Offenders," TechCrunch, December 11, 2019. https://techcrunch.com.
60. Yascha Mounk, "Verboten," *New Republic*, April 3, 2018. https://newrepublic.com.
61. Quoted in Lauren Feiner, "Twitter Users Are Escaping Online Hate by Switching Profiles to Germany, Where Nazism Is Illegal," CNBC, August 3, 2019. www.cnbc.com.

Anti-Defamation League—www.adl.org

The Anti-Defamation League is an anti-hate organization that was founded in 1913. It works toward a future where nobody suffers from discrimination, bias, or hate. The organization's website has numerous maps, charts, and reports about hate, including hate online.

ARTICLE 19—www.article19.org

ARTICLE 19 is an organization that strives to ensure that all people can express themselves freely, without being afraid of discrimination. It believes that hate speech is a form of discrimination and a human rights concern. The organization's website has articles and reports about hate speech around the world.

Dangerous Speech Project—https://dangerousspeech.org

The Dangerous Speech Project investigates how certain types of speech, such as hate speech, can affect violence, and it works to develop effective strategies to prevent that violence. Its website contains numerous publications related to these topics.

Hate in America, News21
https://hateinamerica.news21.com

Hate in America is an investigation by the Carnegie-Knight News21 program. In 2018 reporters interviewed hundreds of people in the United States and reviewed thousands of pages of legal documents in order to get a better understanding of hate in the United States. This website contains numerous articles that reveal their findings.

Southern Poverty Law Center (SPLC)—www.splcenter.org

The SPLC is an organization that is dedicated to fighting bigotry and hate. It monitors hate groups in the United States, teaches tolerance, and seeks justice for the vulnerable. Its website contains numerous reports about hate groups in the United States.

Books

Peter J. Hasson, *The Manipulators: Facebook, Google, Twitter, and Big Tech's War on Conservatives*. Washington, DC: Regnery, 2020.

Michael Miller, *Exposing Hate: Prejudice, Hatred, and Violence in Action*. Minneapolis: Twenty-First Century, 2019.

Sue Scheff, *Shame Nation: The Global Epidemic of Online Hate*. Naperville, IL: Sourcebooks, 2017.

Frederik Stjernfelt, *Your Post Has Been Removed: Tech Giants and Freedom of Speech*. Cham, Switzerland: SpringerOpen, 2020.

Nicolas P. Suzor, *Lawless: The Secret Rules That Govern Our Digital Lives*. New York: Cambridge University Press, 2019.

Internet Sources

Anti-Defamation League, "Online Hate and Harassment: The American Experience," 2018. www.adl.org.

Amitai Etzioni, "My Experience with Social Media Restrictions on Free Speech," *National Interest*, December 15, 2019. https://nationalinterest.org.

Rachel Hatzipanagos, "How Online Hate Turns into Real-Life Violence," *Washington Post*, November 30, 2018. www.washingtonpost.com.

Kate Klonick, "The New Governors: The People, Rules, and Processes Governing Online Speech," *Harvard Law Review*, April 2018. https://harvardlawreview.org.

Zachary Laub, "Hate Speech on Social Media: Global Comparisons," Council on Foreign Relations, June 7, 2019. www.cfr.org.

Nadine Strossen, "Counterspeech in Response to Changing Notions of Free Speech," American Bar Association. www.americanbar.org.

US Department of Justice, "2018 Hate Crime Statistics." www.justice.gov.

Niam Yaraghi, "How Should Social Media Platforms Combat Misinformation and Hate Speech?," *TechTank* (blog), Brookings Institution, April 9, 2019. www.brookings.edu.

Cover: Shutterstock.com

5: AP Photo/Mahesh Kumar A.
10: Adwo/Shutterstock.com
13: mooremedia/Shutterstock.com
17: TheVisualsYouNeed/Shutterstock.com
21: Fadhli Adnan/Shutterstock.com
24: Maury Aaseng
27: LightField Studios/Shutterstock.com
33: vkilikov/Shutterstock.com
34: Twin Design/Shutterstock.com
38: Kaspars Grinvalds/Shutterstock.com
44: fizkes/Shutterstock.com
47: JeremyRichards/Shutterstock.com
49: JStone/Shutterstock.com